THIS WALKER BOOK BELONGS TO:

_____

Acknowledgements
With the exception of Lewis Carroll,
Hilaire Belloc and Edward Lear, the authors
of the rhymes in this book are unknown.
Thanks are due for permission to reprint the following
copyright material: "The Elephant" by Hilaire Belloc
(published in Selected Cautionary Verses, Puffin 1987)
reprinted by permission of the Peters, Fraser
and Dunlop Group Ltd.

First published 1990 by Walker Books Ltd
87 Vauxhall Walk, London SE11 5HJ

This edition published 2000

2 4 6 8 10 9 7 5 3 1

Illustrations © 1990 Emma Chichester Clark

This book has been typeset in Plantin.

Printed in Hong Kong

British Library Cataloguing in Publication Data
A catalogue record for this book is
available from the British Library.

ISBN 0-7445-7753-5

I Never Saw a Purple Cow

and other nonsense poems

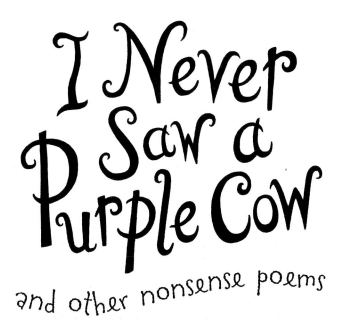

Emma Chichester Clark

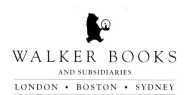

WALKER BOOKS

AND SUBSIDIARIES

LONDON • BOSTON • SYDNEY

For Will

A CAT CAME FIDDLING

A cat came fiddling out of a barn,
With a pair of bag-pipes under her arm;
She could sing nothing but Fiddle cum fee,
The mouse has married the bumble-bee.
Pipe, cat; dance, mouse;
We'll have a wedding at our good house.

THE OWL AND THE PUSSY-CAT

The Owl and the Pussy-cat went to sea
   In a beautiful pea-green boat;
They took some honey, and plenty of money,
   Wrapped up in a five-pound note.
The Owl looked up to the stars above,
   And sang to a small guitar,
"O lovely Pussy! O Pussy, my love,
   What a beautiful Pussy you are,
      You are,
      You are!
   What a beautiful Pussy you are!"

Pussy said to the Owl, "You elegant fowl!
    How charmingly sweet you sing!
O let us be married! too long we have tarried:
    But what shall we do for a ring?"
They sailed away, for a year and a day,
    To the land where the Bong-tree grows,
And there in a wood a Piggy-wig stood,
    With a ring at the end of his nose,
        His nose,
        His nose,
    With a ring at the end of his nose.

"Dear Pig, are you willing to sell for one shilling
    Your ring?" Said the Piggy, "I will."
So they took it away, and were married next day
    By the Turkey who lives on the hill.
They dined on mince, and slices of quince,
    Which they ate with a runcible spoon;
And hand in hand, on the edge of the sand,
    They danced by the light of the moon,
        The moon,
        The moon,
    They danced by the light of the moon.

Edward Lear

SING, SING

Sing, sing,
    What shall I sing?
The cat's run away
    With the pudding string!
Do, do,
    What shall I do?
The cat's run away
    With the pudding too!

THE CAT SAT ASLEEP

The cat sat asleep by the side of the fire,
    The mistress snored loud as a pig;
Jack took up his fiddle by Jenny's desire,
    And struck up a bit of a jig.

THERE WAS AN OLD PERSON OF BRAY

There was an Old Person of Bray,
Who sang through the whole of the Day
   To his Ducks and his Pigs,
   Whom he fed upon Figs,
That valuable Person of Bray.

Edward Lear

THERE WAS A YOUNG LADY OF BUTE

There was a Young Lady of Bute,
Who played on a silver-gilt flute;
She played several jigs
To her uncle's white pigs,
   That amusing Young Lady of Bute.

Edward Lear

THERE WAS AN OLD MAN ON THE BORDER

There was an Old Man on the Border,
Who lived in the utmost disorder;
He danced with the Cat
And made Tea in his Hat,
   Which vexed all the folks on the Border.

Edward Lear

11

THE ELEPHANT IS A GRACEFUL BIRD

The elephant is a graceful bird;
  It flits from twig to twig.
It builds its nest in a rhubarb tree
  And whistles like a pig.

WAY DOWN SOUTH

Way down South where bananas grow,
A grasshopper stepped on an elephant's toe.
The elephant said, with tears in his eyes,
"Pick on somebody your own size."

THE ELEPHANT

When people call this beast to mind,
  They marvel more and more
At such a LITTLE tail behind,
So LARGE a trunk before.

Hilaire Belloc

DICKERY, DICKERY, DARE

Dickery, dickery, dare,
The pig flew up in the air;
The man in brown
Soon brought him down,
Dickery, dickery, dare.

LITTLE JACK SPRAT

Little Jack Sprat
    Once had a pig;
It was not very little,
    Nor yet very big,
It was not very lean,
    It was not very fat –
It's a good pig to grunt,
    Said little Jack Sprat.

THE PETTITOES

The pettitoes are little feet,
    And the little feet not big;
Great feet belong to the grunting hog,
    And the pettitoes to the little pig.

AS I LOOKED OUT

As I looked out on Saturday last,
A fat little pig went hurrying past.
Over his shoulders he wore a shawl,
Although he didn't seem cold at all.
I waved at him, but he didn't see,
For he never so much as looked at me.
Once again, when the moon was high,
I saw the little pig hurrying by;
Back he came at a terrible pace,
The moonlight shone on his little pink face,
And he smiled with a face that was quite content.
But never I knew where that little pig went.

WHOSE LITTLE PIGS

Whose little pigs are these, these, these?
    Whose little pigs are these?
They are Roger the Cook's, I know by their looks;
    I found them among my peas.
Go pound them, go pound them.
    I dare not on my life,
For though I love not Roger the Cook,
    I dearly love his wife.

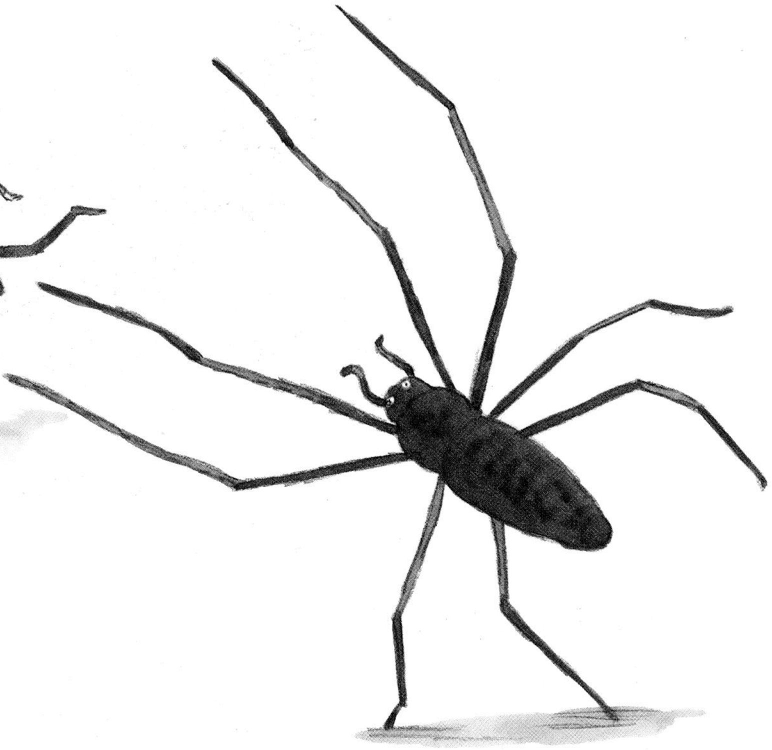

TEASING

Little Jack Horner
Sat in the corner,
Eating his curds and whey;
There came a big spider,
Who sat down beside her,
And the dish ran away with the spoon.

LITTLE MISS TUCKETT

Little Miss Tuckett
Sat on a bucket,
Eating some peaches and cream;
There came a grasshopper
And tried hard to stop her
But she said, "Go away, or I'll scream."

16

LITTLE POLL PARROT

Little Poll Parrot
Sat in his garret
Eating toast and tea;
A little brown mouse
Jumped into the house,
And stole it all away.

LITTLE TIM SPRAT

Little Tim Sprat
Had a pet rat,
In a tin cage with a wheel.
Said little Tim Sprat,
Each day to his rat:
If hungry, my dear, you must squeal.

A RABBIT RACED A TURTLE

A rabbit raced a turtle,
You know the turtle won;
And Mister Bunny came in late –
A little hot cross bun.

POOR DOG BRIGHT

Poor dog Bright
Ran off with all his might
Because the cat was after him
Poor dog Bright.

Poor cat Fright
Ran off with all her might
Because the dog was after her
Poor cat Fright.

RATS IN THE GARDEN

Rats in the garden, catch 'em Towser,
Cows in the cornfield, run, boys, run;
Cat's in the cream pot, stop her, now sir,
Fire on the mountain, run, boys, run.

19

THERE WAS AN OLD SOLDIER OF BISTER

There was an old soldier of Bister
Went walking one day with his sister,
   When a cow at one poke
   Tossed her into an oak
Before the old gentleman missed her.

A FUNNY OLD PERSON

A funny old person of Slough
Took all of his meals with a cow.
   He said, "It's uncanny,
   She's so like Aunt Fanny!"
But he never would indicate how.

RAT A TAT TAT

Rat a tat tat, who is that?
Only grandma's pussy cat.
What do you want?
A pint of milk.
Where's your money?
In my pocket.
Where's your pocket?
I forgot it.
O you silly pussy cat.

A LIZARD WRIGGLED

A lizard wriggled on his belly
To Leeds to see his Aunt Nelly.
She said, "What a long, long way you've come,
A-wriggling on your tired tum."

CALICO PIE

Calico Pie,
The little Birds fly
Down to the calico tree,
Their wings were blue,
And they sang "Tilly-loo!"
Till away they flew –
And they never came back to me!
They never came back!
They never came back!
They never came back to me!

Calico Jam,
The little Fish swam,
Over the syllabub sea,
He took off his hat,
To the Sole and the Sprat,
And the Willeby-wat –
But he never came back to me!
He never came back!
He never came back!
He never came back to me!

Calico Ban,
 The little Mice ran,
To be ready in time for tea,
 Flippity flup,
 They drank it all up,
 And danced in the cup –
But they never came back to me!
 They never came back!
 They never came back!
They never came back to me!

Calico Drum,
 The Grasshoppers come,
The Butterfly, Beetle and Bee,
 Over the ground,
 Around and round,
 With a hop and a bound –
But they never came back!
 They never came back!
 They never came back!
They never came back to me!

Edward Lear

23

THE ANIMAL FAIR

I went to the animal fair,
The birds and beasts were there.
The big baboon, by the light of the moon,
Was combing his auburn hair.
The monkey, he got drunk,
And sat on the elephant's trunk.
The elephant sneezed and fell on his knees,
And what became of the monk, the monk?

LEG OVER LEG

Leg over leg.
   As the dog went to Dover,
When he came to a stile,
   Jump – he went over.

TWO LITTLE DOGS

   Two little dogs
   Sat by the fire
Over a fender of coal dust;
   Said one little dog
   To the other little dog,
If you don't talk, why, I must.

THERE WAS A YOUNG MAN

There was a young man of Bengal
Who went to a fancy-dress ball,
He went, just for fun,
Dressed up as a bun,
And a dog ate him up in the hall.

AN OLD GREY HORSE

An old grey horse stood on the wall,
As daft as he was high.
He had no fear of falling down,
He thought he was a fly.

WHOOPS!

A horse and a flea and three blind mice
Sat on a curbstone shooting dice.
The horse he slipped and fell on the flea.
The flea said, "Whoops, there's a horse on me."

LITTLE FLY

Little fly upon the wall,
Ain't you got no clothes at all?
Ain't you got no shimmy shirt?
Ain't you got no petti-skirt?
Brrrrrr! Ain't you cold?

A BUG AND A FLEA

A bug and a flea
Went to sea
On a reel of cotton.
The bug was drowned
The flea was found
Stuck to a mermaid's bottom.

PUSSY SITS BESIDE THE FIRE

Pussy sits beside the fire,
    So pretty and so fair.
In walks the little dog,
    Ah, pussy, are you there?
How do you do, Mistress Pussy?
    Mistress Pussy, how do you do?
I thank you kindly, little dog,
    I'm very well just now.

I HAD A LITTLE HEN

I had a little hen,
    The prettiest ever seen;
She washed up the dishes,
    And kept the house clean.
She went to the mill
    To fetch me some flour,
And always got home
    In less than an hour.
She baked me my bread,
    She brewed me my ale,
She sat by the fire
    And told a fine tale.

DAME TROT AND HER CAT

Dame Trot and her cat
Sat down for to chat;
The Dame sat on this side,
And Puss sat on that.

"Puss," says the Dame,
"Can you catch a rat,
Or a mouse in the dark?"
"Purr," says the cat.

THE SOW CAME IN

The sow came in with the saddle,
The little pig rocked the cradle,
    The dish jumped up on the table,
    To see the pot swallow the ladle.
The spit that stood behind the door
Threw the pudding-stick on the floor.
    Odd's-bobs! says the gridiron,
        Can't you agree?
    I'm the head constable,
        Bring them to me.

FUZZY WUZZY

Fuzzy Wuzzy was a bear;
Fuzzy Wuzzy had no hair.
So Fuzzy Wuzzy wasn't fuzzy. Was he?

THREE GREY GEESE

Three grey geese in a green field grazing
Grey were the geese and green was the grazing.

ALGY MET A BEAR

Algy met a bear,
A bear met Algy.
The bear was bulgy,
The bulge was Algy.

THERE WAS AN OLD MAN OF DUMBREE

There was an Old Man of Dumbree,
Who taught little Owls to drink Tea;
For he said, "To eat mice
Is not proper or nice,"
    That amiable Man of Dumbree.

Edward Lear

THERE WAS AN OLD MAN WITH A BEARD

There was an Old Man with a beard
Who said, "It is just as I feared! –
    Four Larks and a Wren,
    Two Owls and a Hen,
Have all built their nests in my beard!"

Edward Lear

THERE WAS AN OLD MAN WHO SAID

There was an Old Man who said, "How
Shall I flee from that horrible cow?
I will sit on this stile
And continue to smile,
    Which may soften the heart of that cow."

Edward Lear

THE PURPLE COW

I never saw a purple cow,
I never hope to see one;
But I can tell you, any how,
I'd rather see than be one.

THE QUANGLE WANGLE'S HAT

On the top of the Crumpetty Tree
    The Quangle Wangle sat,
But his face you could not see,
    On account of his Beaver Hat.
For his Hat was a hundred and two feet wide,
    With ribbons and bibbons on every side
And bells, and buttons, and loops, and lace,
    So that nobody ever could see the face
    Of the Quangle Wangle Quee.

The Quangle Wangle said
    To himself on the Crumpetty Tree, –
"Jam; and jelly; and bread;
    "Are the best food for me!
"But the longer I live on this Crumpetty Tree,
"The plainer than ever it seems to me
"That very few people come this way
"And that life on the whole is far from gay!"
    Said the Quangle Wangle Quee.

But there came to the Crumpetty Tree,
    Mr and Mrs Canary;
And they said – "Did you ever see
    "Any spot so charmingly airy?
"May we build a nest on your lovely Hat?
"Mr Quangle Wangle, grant us that!
"O please let us come and build a nest
"Of whatever material suits you best,
    "Mr Quangle Wangle Quee!"

And besides, to the Crumpetty Tree
   Came the Stork, the Duck, and the Owl;
The Snail, and the Bumble-Bee,
   The Frog, and the Fimble Fowl;
   (The Fimble Fowl, with a Corkscrew leg);
And all of them said, – "We humbly beg,
   "We may build our homes on your lovely Hat, –
   "Mr Quangle Wangle, grant us that!
   "Mr Quangle Wangle Quee!"

And the Golden Grouse came there,
   And the Pobble who has no toes, –
And the small Olympian bear, –
   And the Dong with a luminous nose.
And the Blue Baboon, who played the flute, –
And the Orient Calf from the Land of Tute, –
And the Attery Squash, and the Bisky Bat, –
All came and built on the lovely Hat
   Of the Quangle Wangle Quee.

And the Quangle Wangle said
   To himself on the Crumpetty Tree –
"When all these creatures move
   "What a wonderful noise there'll be!"
And at night by the light of the Mulberry moon
They danced to the Flute of the Blue Baboon,
On the broad green leaves of the Crumpetty Tree,
And all were as happy as happy could be,
   With the Quangle Wangle Quee.

Edward Lear

THE MONKEY AND THE DONKEY

Said the monkey to the donkey,
"What'll you have to drink?"
Said the donkey to the monkey,
"I'd like a swig of ink."

OLD-JUMPETY-BUMPETY-HOP-AND-GO-ONE

Old-Jumpety-Bumpety-Hop-and-Go-One
Was lying on his side in the sun.
This old kangaroo, he was whisking the flies
(With his glossy tail) from his ears and his eyes.
Jumpety-Bumpety-Hop-and-Go-One
Was lying asleep on his side in the sun,
Jumpety-Bumpety-Hop!

THE CROCODILE

How doth the little crocodile
  Improve his shining tail,
And pour the waters of the Nile
  On every golden scale!

How cheerfully he seems to grin!
  How neatly spread his claws,
And welcomes little fishes in
  With gently smiling jaws!

Lewis Carroll

THREE YOUNG RATS

Three young rats with black felt hats,
Three young ducks with white straw flats,
Three young dogs with curling tails,
Three young cats with demi-veils,
Went out to walk with two young pigs
In satin vests and sorrel wigs;
But suddenly it chanced to rain,
And so they all went home again.

BAT, BAT

Bat, bat,
    Come under my hat,
  And I'll give you a slice of bacon;
And when I bake,
I'll give you a cake,
  If I am not mistaken.

HE WAS A RAT, AND SHE WAS A RAT

He was a rat, and she was a rat,
And down in one hole they did dwell,
And both were as black as a witch's cat,
And they loved each other well.

He had a tail, and she had a tail,
Both long and curling and fine;
And each said, "Yours is the finest tail
In the world, excepting mine."

He smelt the cheese, and she smelt the cheese,
And they both pronounced it good;
And both remarked it would greatly add
To the charms of their daily food.

So he ventured out, and she ventured out,
And I saw them go with pain;
But what befell them I never can tell,
For they never came back again.

Index of first lines

I Never Saw A Purple Cow

EMMA CHICHESTER CLARK thoroughly enjoys the silliness
of the nonsense rhymes in *I Never Saw A Purple Cow*.
She says, "I love nonsense poems and most of these poems have
no sense at all. They are zany and wacky and a great excuse
to draw as many animals as possible."

Emma Chichester Clark trained at the Chelsea School of Art and
the Royal College of Art. Since 1983 she has worked as a freelance
illustrator for magazines and for both children's and adults' books.

Emma won first prize in the Folio Society's Awards at the
Royal College of Art, and second prize in the Benson and Hedges
Gold Awards for Illustration. She won the 1987 Mother Goose
Award for *Listen to This* and has since illustrated several children's
books, including *I Love You, Blue Kangaroo!* (which she also
wrote), which was shortlisted for the Kate Greenaway Medal.
Emma lives in London.

Some more verse collections from Walker

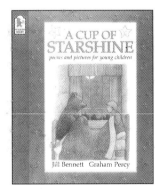

ISBN 0-7445-6097-7 (pb)

ISBN 0-7445-3161-6 (pb)

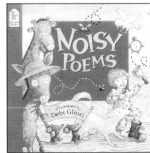

ISBN 0-7445-6996-6 (pb)

ISBN 0-7445-5498-5 (pb)